Amazing Dogs

Adult Coloring Book

By

Blush Design

Hi there!

I am the founder of Blush Design, a small business dedicated to bringing joy and relaxation to the world.

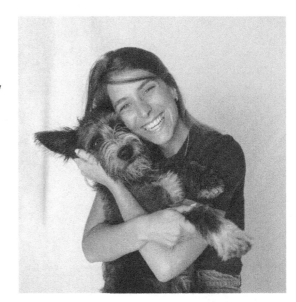

Our mission is simple – to create beautifully designed coloring books that people can get lost in at the end of a long hard day.

I appreciate your support in buying this book, and would love to share more of our coloring books with you.

Whether you're looking for relaxing or inspirational, rude or simply hilarious, there's a design to match your every mood!

Head on over to our Amazon store for more:

Love,

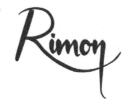

Amazing Dogs \ Blush Design

ISBN-13: 978-1518621680
ISBN-10: 1518621686

Contact Information: agency@ebook-pro.com
Publisher: www.ebook-pro.com

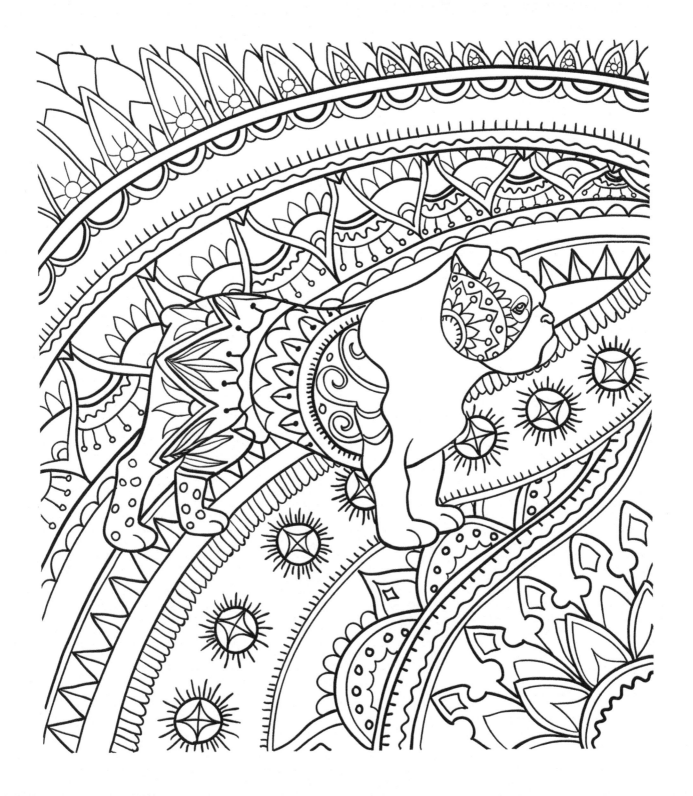

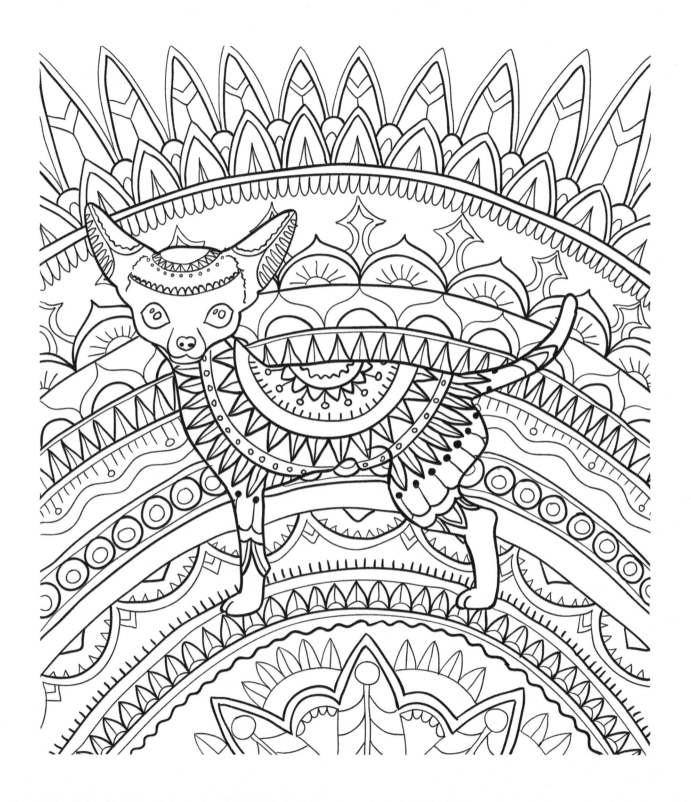

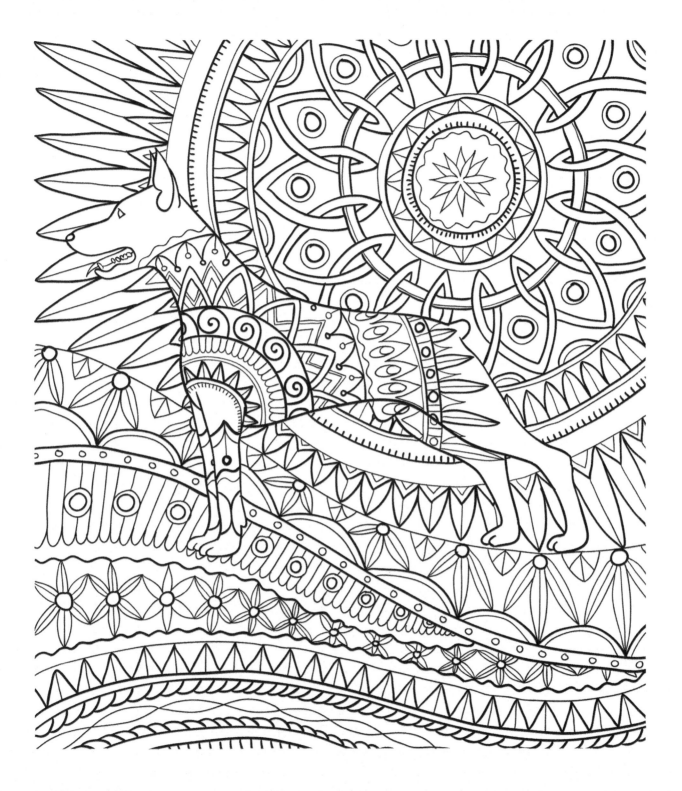

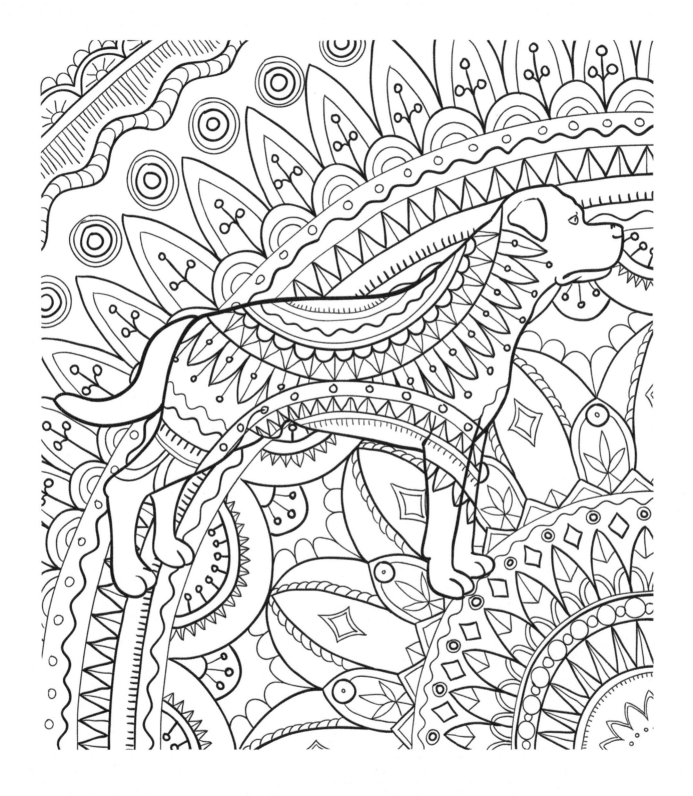

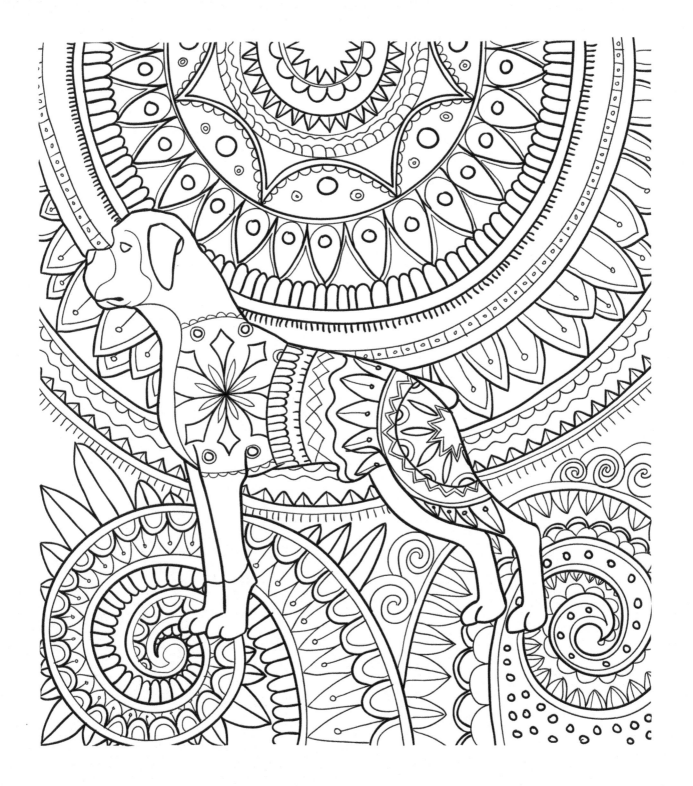

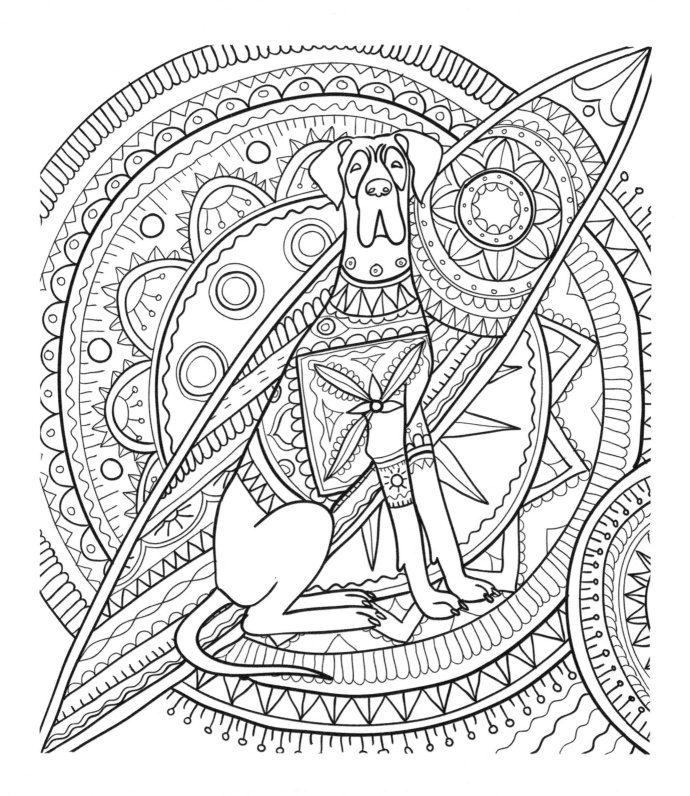

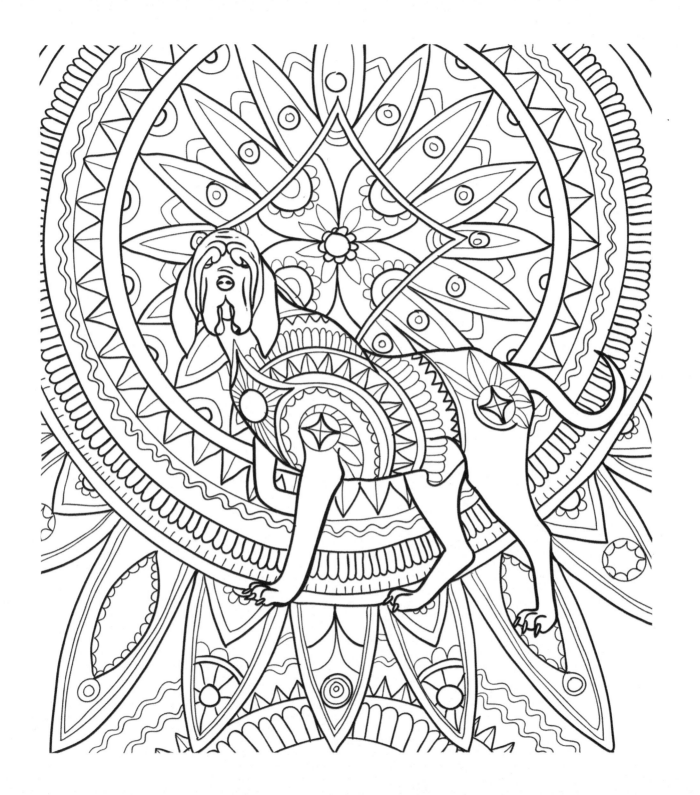

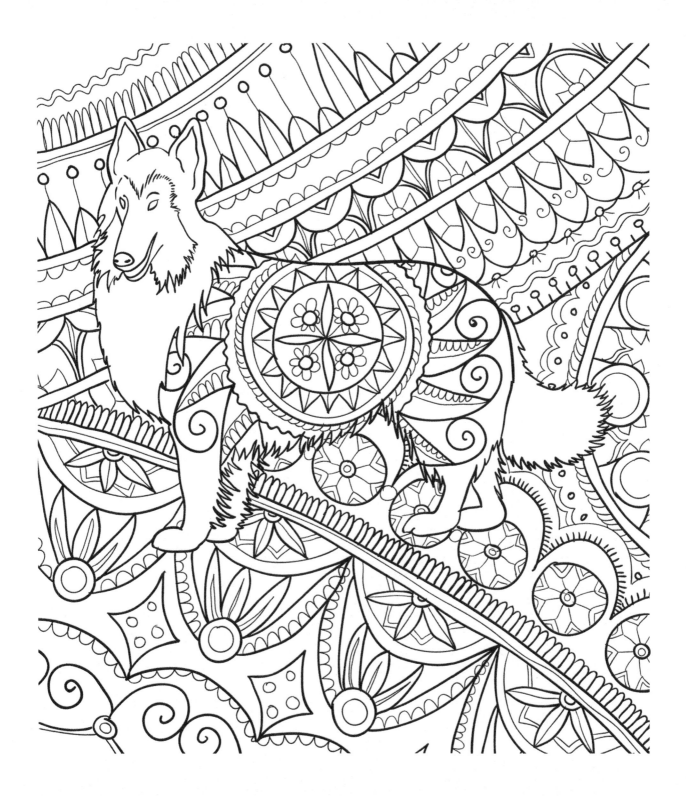

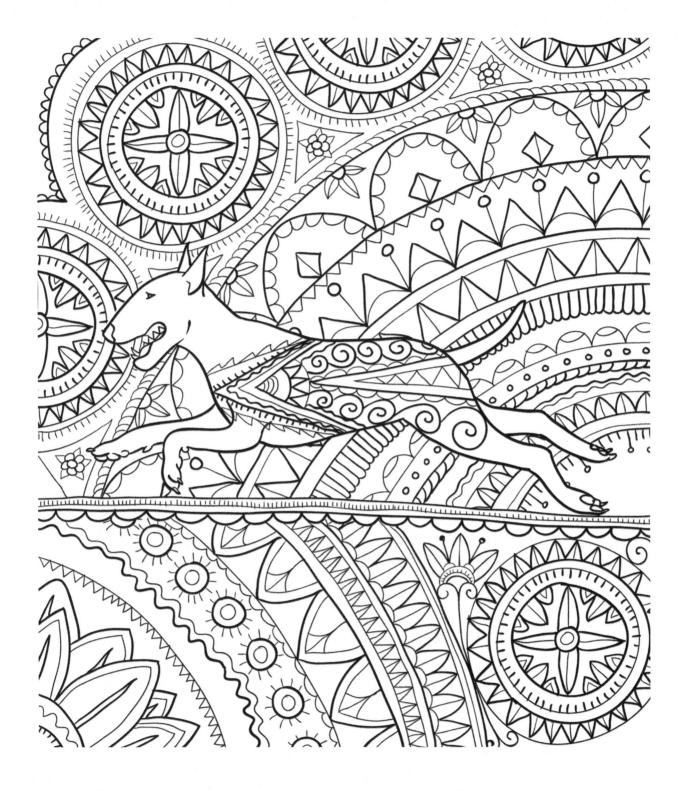

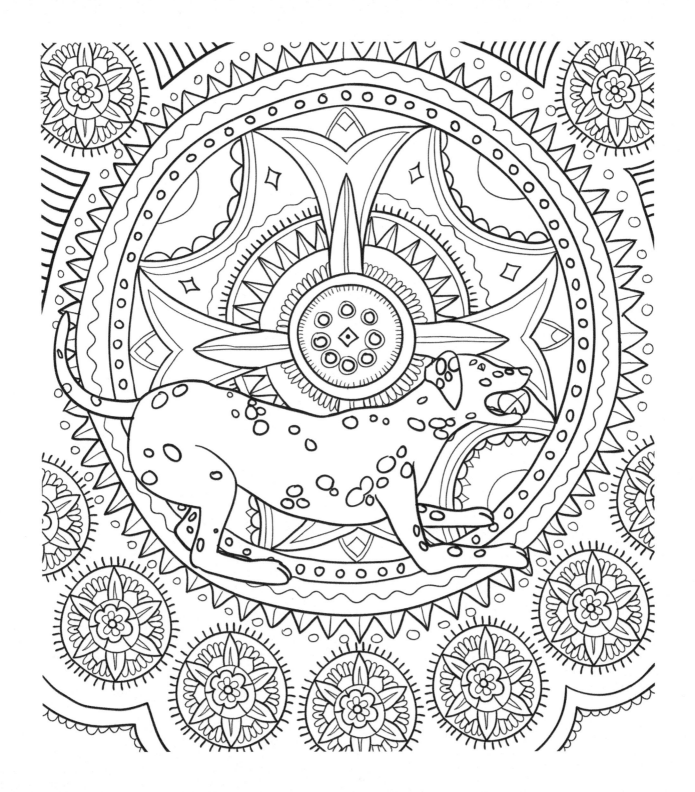

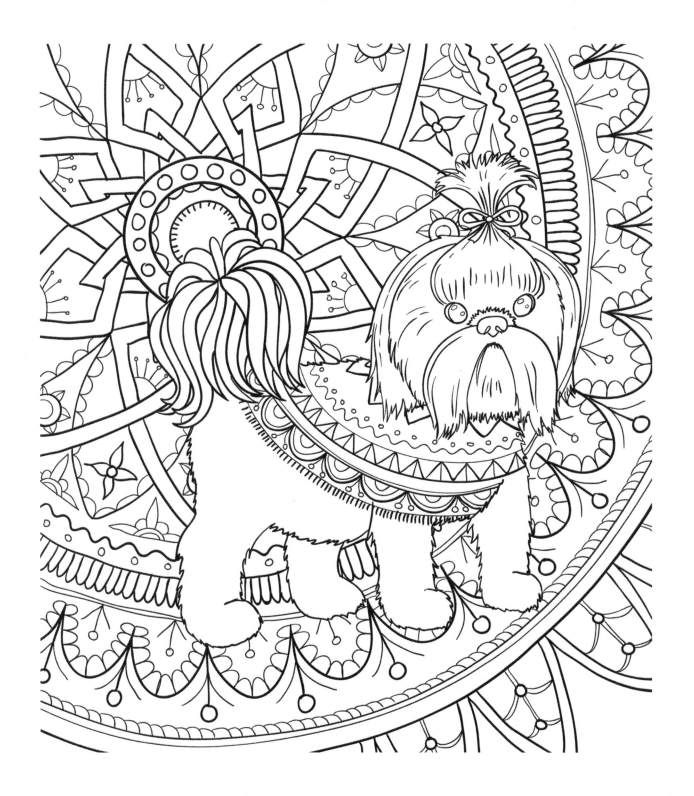

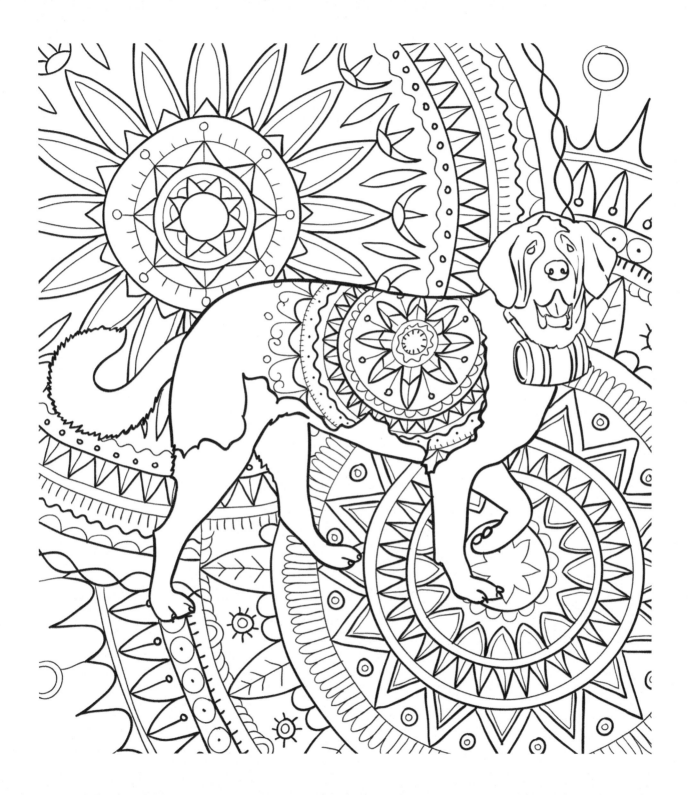

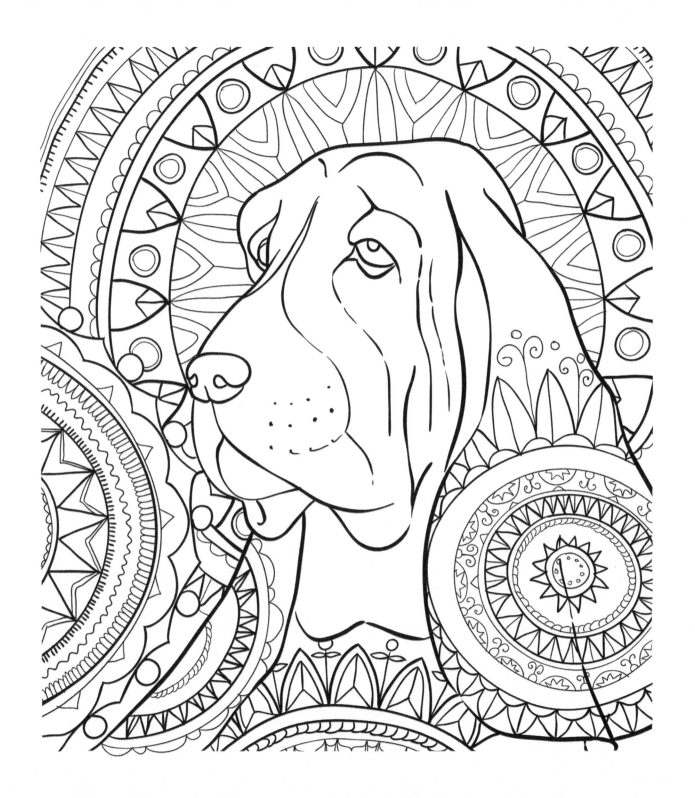

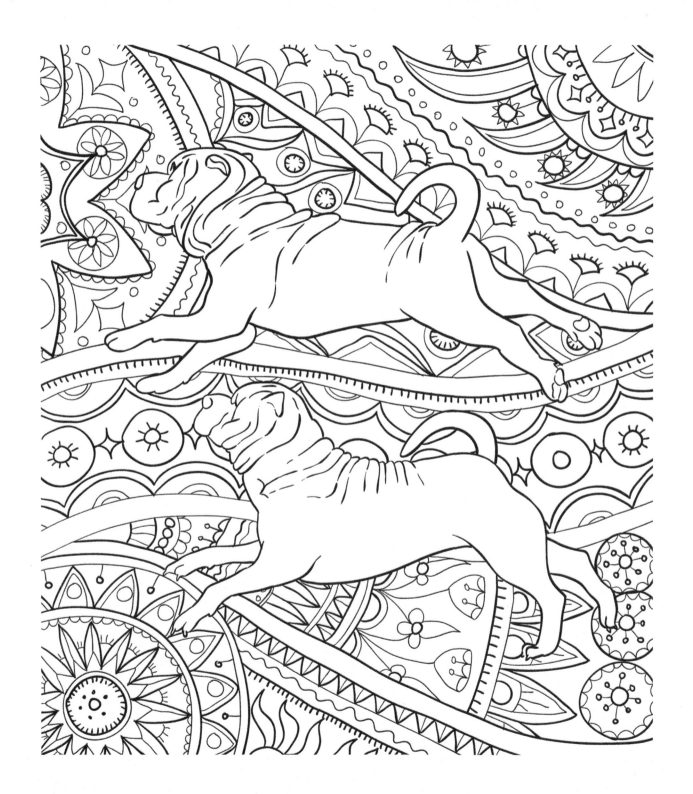

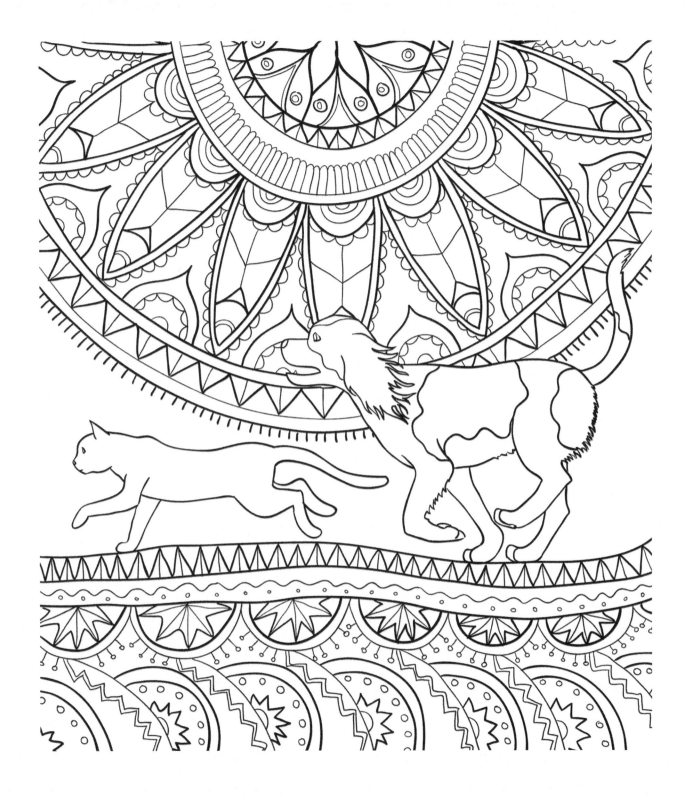

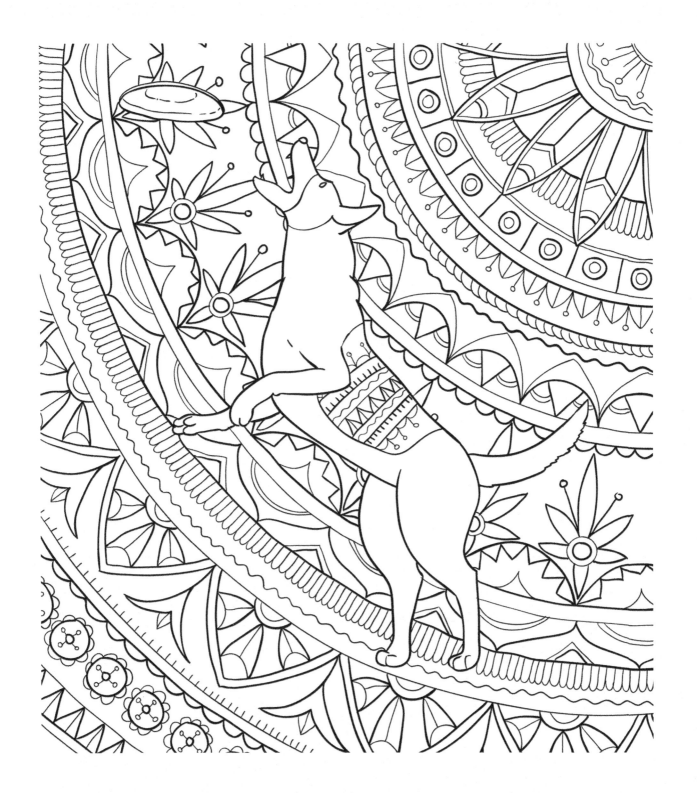

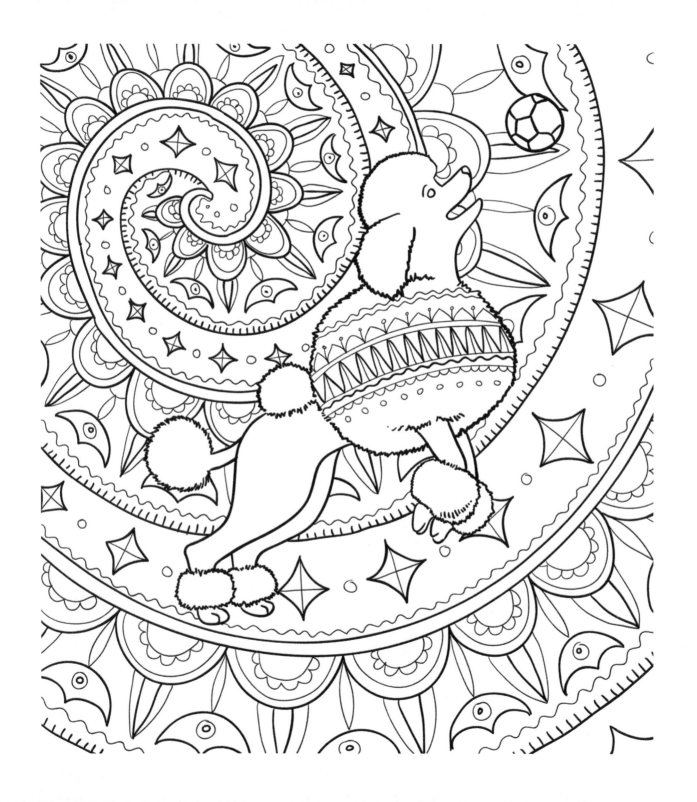

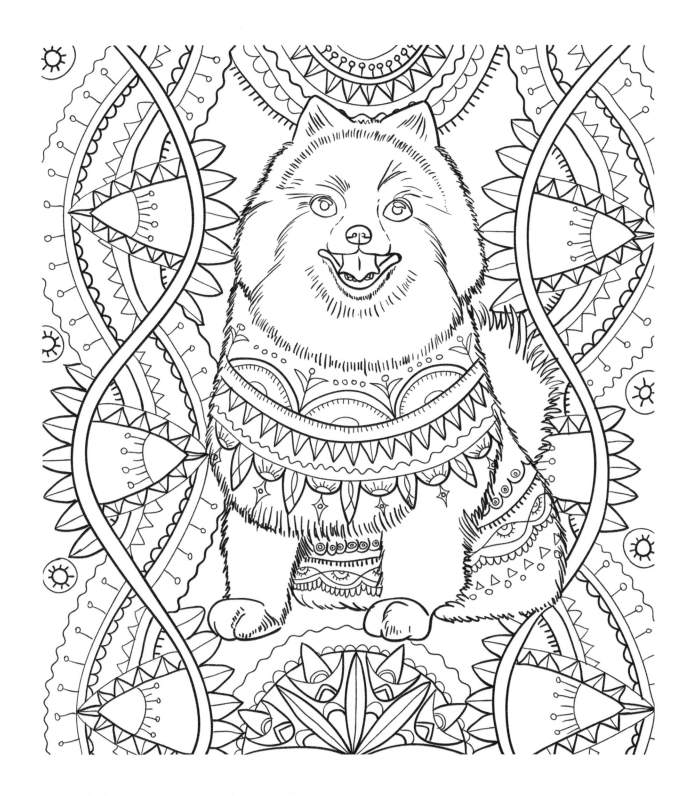

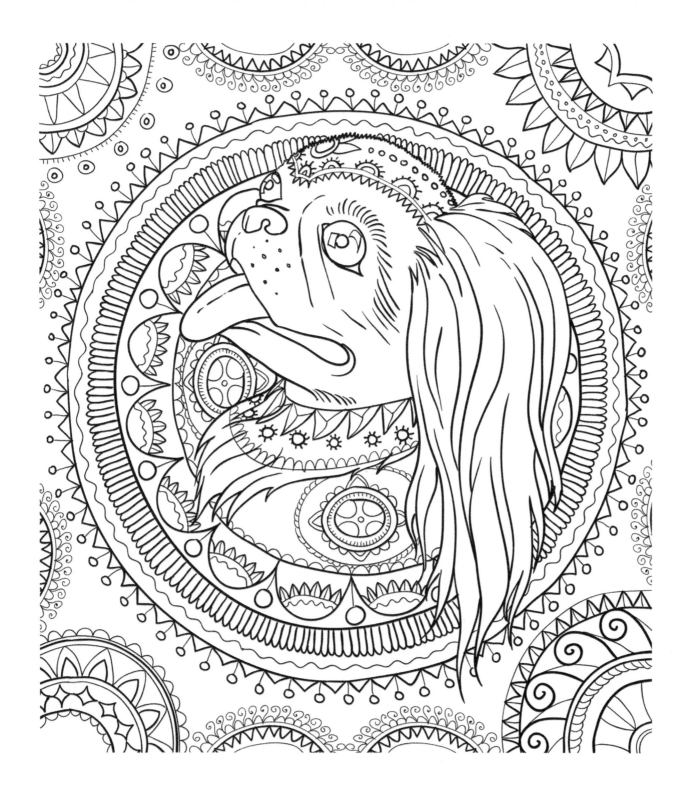

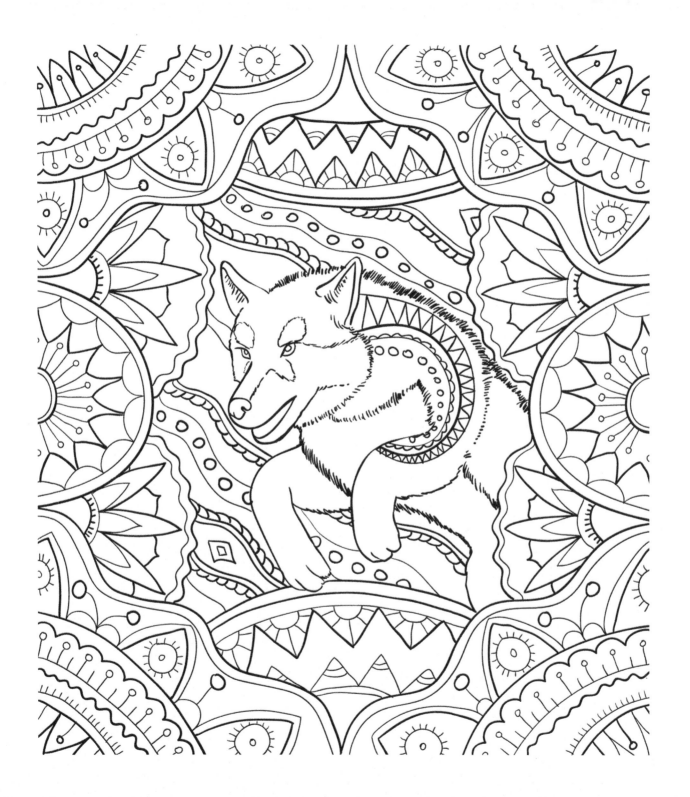

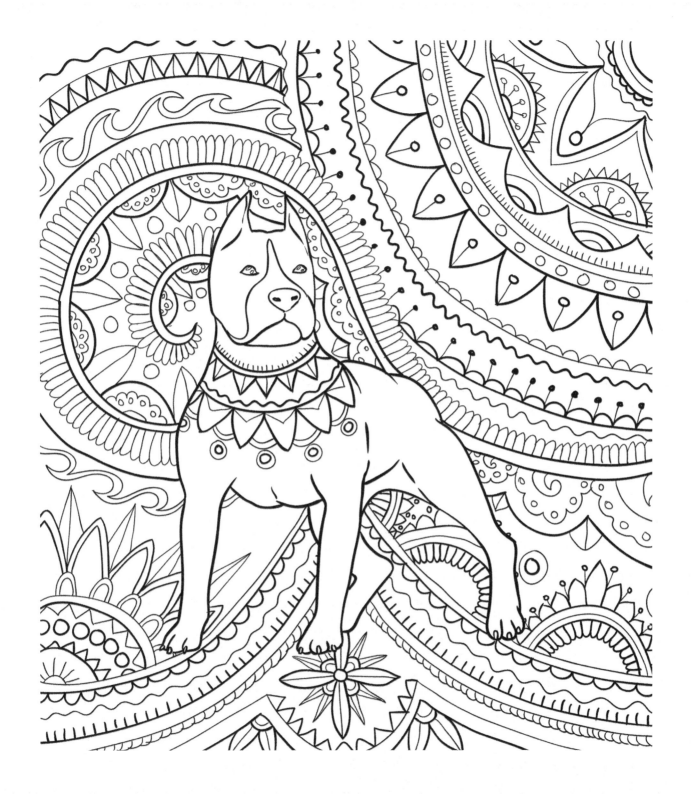

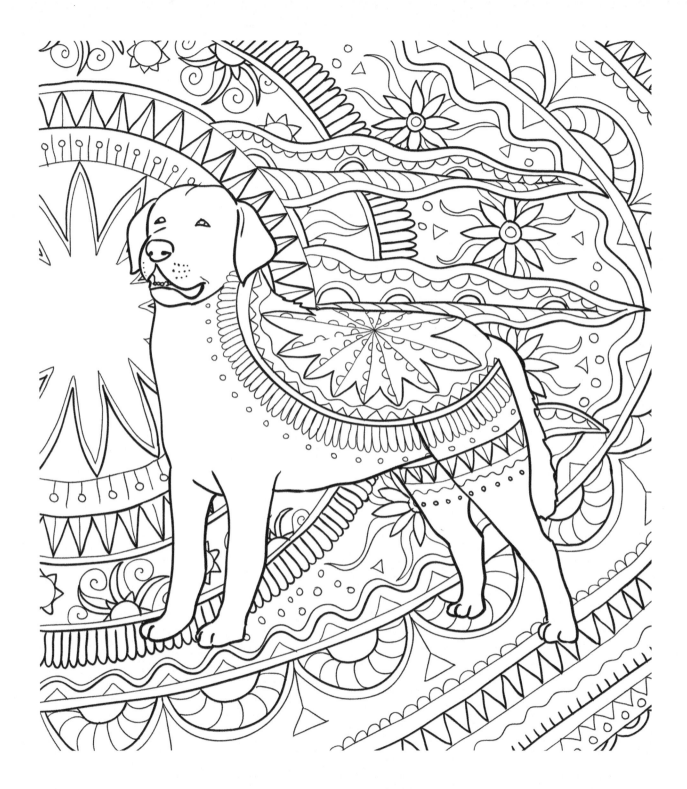

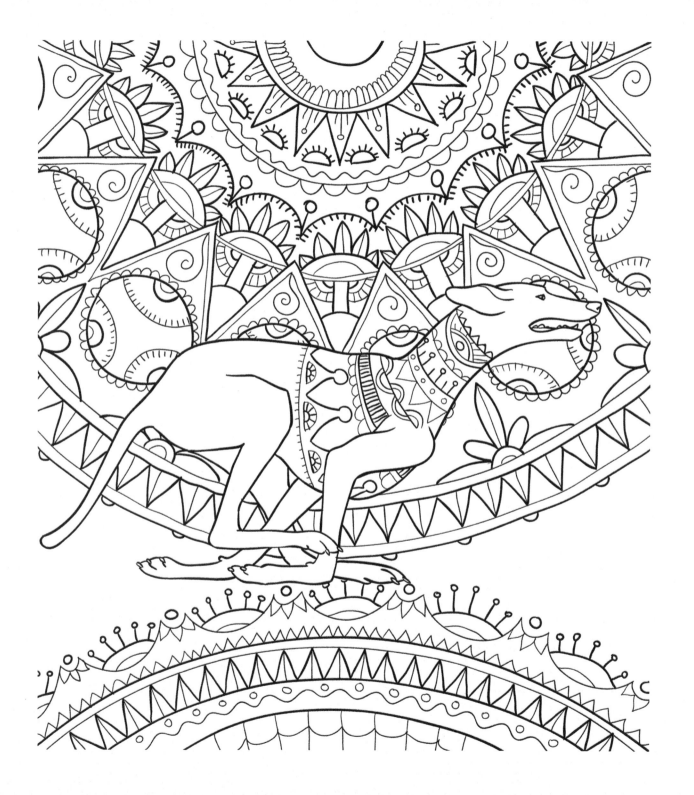

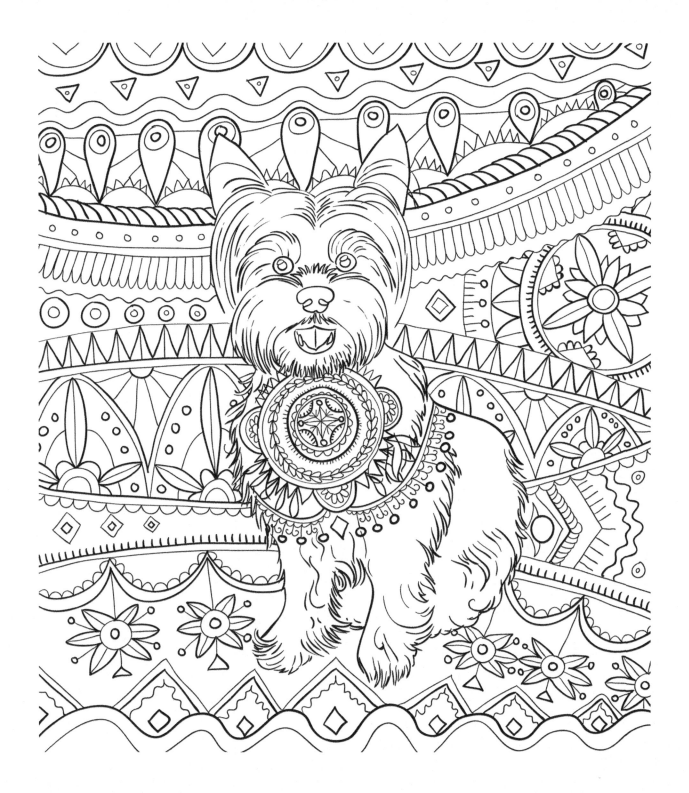

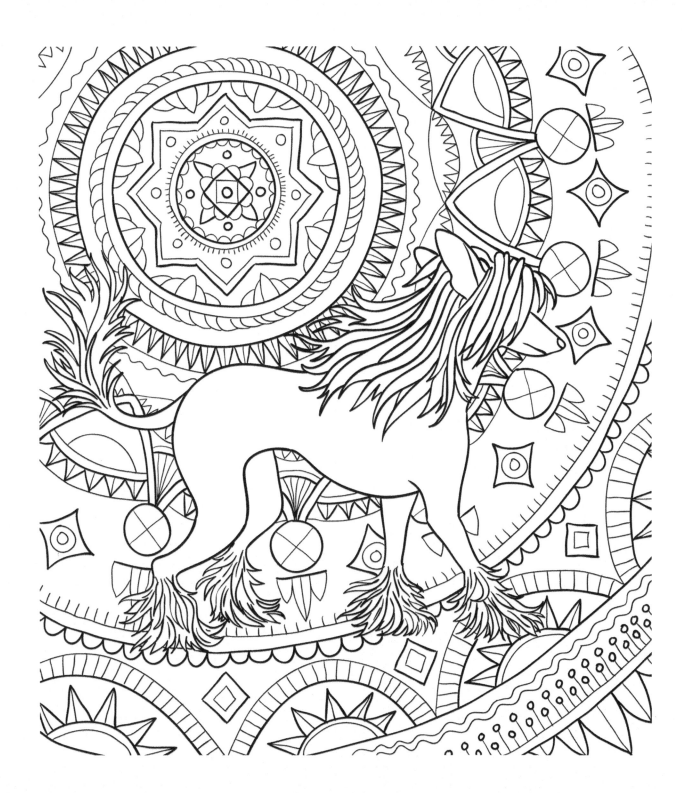

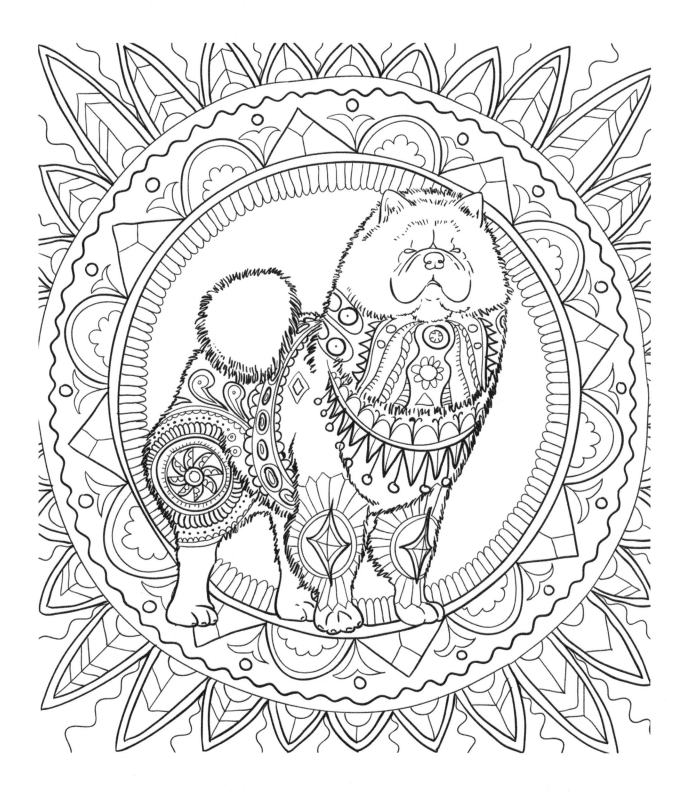

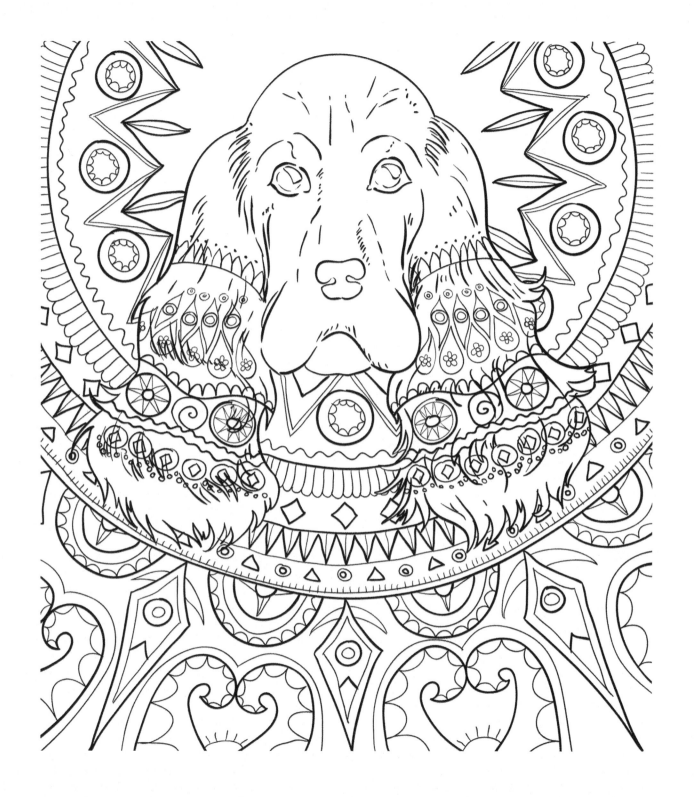

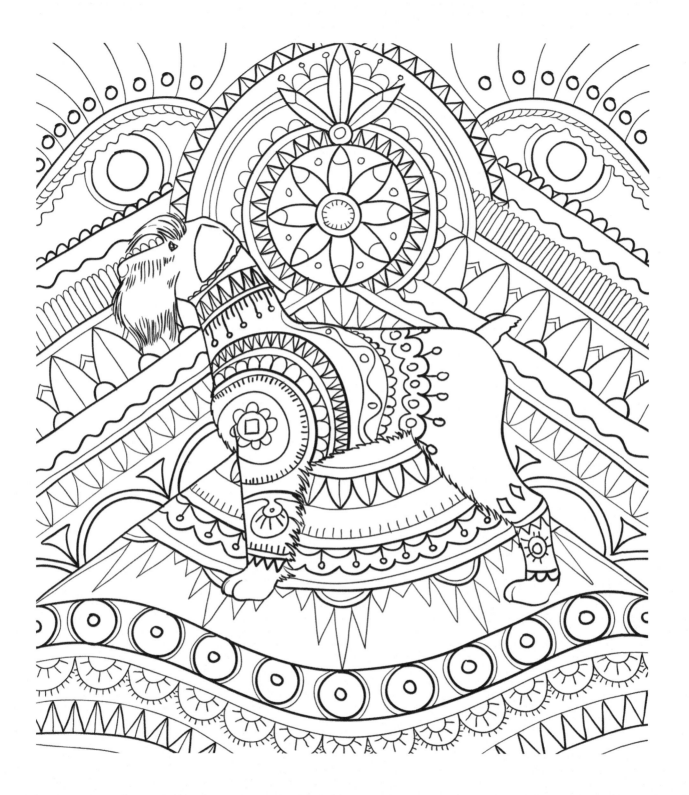

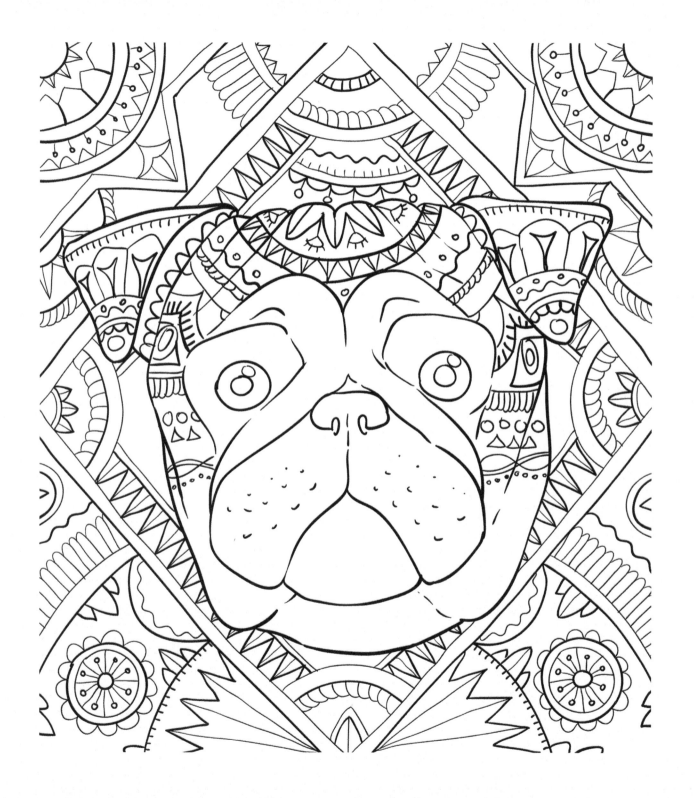

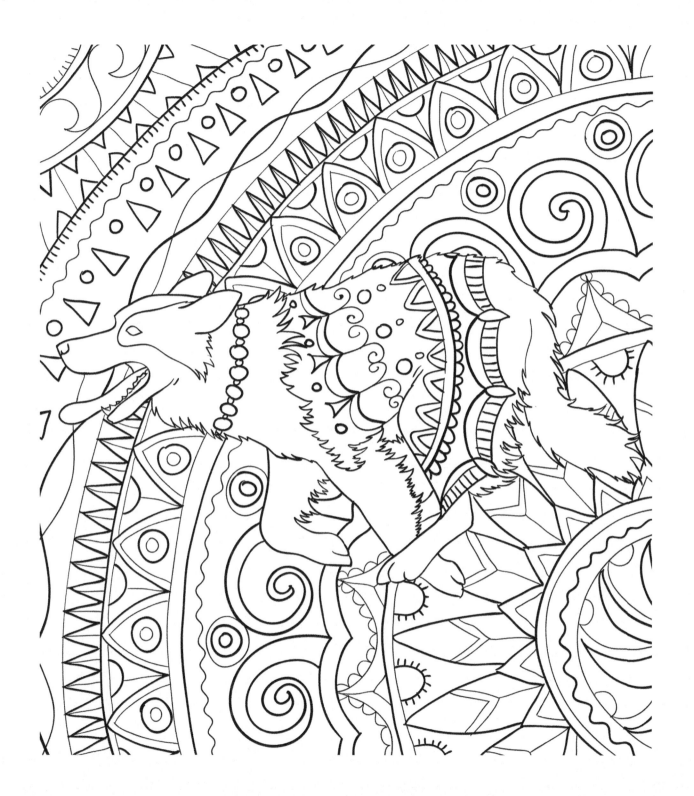

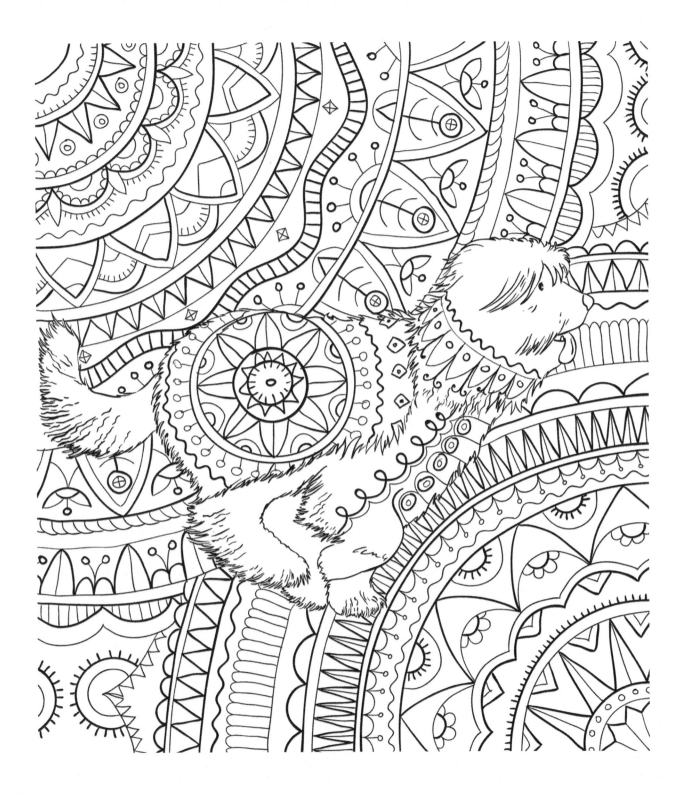

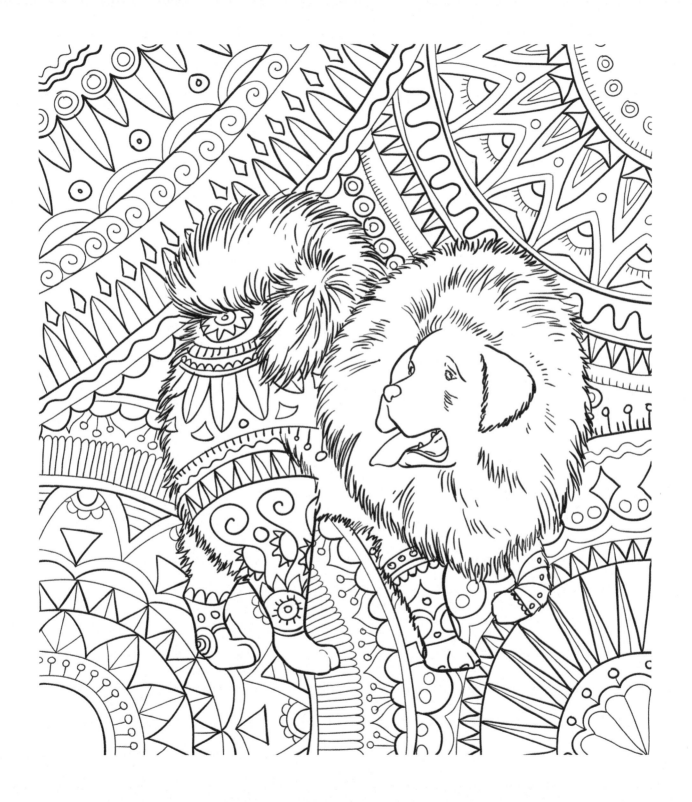

List of Pictures:

1. Bulldog
2. Chihuahua
3. Doberman
4. Rottweiler
5. Boxer
6. Great Danish
7. Bloodhound dog
8. Collie
9. Bull Terrier
10. Dalmatian Dog
11. Shih Tzu
12. San Bernard
13. Basset Hound
14. Shar Pei
15. King Charles
16. German Shepherd
17. Poodle
18. Pomeranian
19. Pekingese
20. Husky
21. American Staffordshire Terrier (Amstaff)
22. Labrador Retriever
23. Greyhound
24. Yorkshire Terrier
25. Chinese Crested Dog
26. Chow Chow
27. Cocker Spaniel
28. Schnauzer
29. Pug
30. Herding dog
31. Old English Sheepdog
32. Red Chinese Tibetan Mastiff

Dear coloring enthusiast,

Thank you for purchasing this book!
We really hope you enjoyed coloring these designs, they were created with much love.

For more beautiful coloring pages like these, visit our Amazon store here:

SCAN ME

We love reading the reviews posted on Amazon and seeing the beautiful colored pictures people upload.
So PLEASE post a review on Amazon for this book.

You are more than welcome to join and share your paintings through our Facebook page **blush design art** and through Instagram **blush.design.art**

P.S
What would you like to color next? You are invited to suggest a topic for our next coloring book.
You can send us an email to agency@ebook-pro.com
We answer all our emails.

Blush Design

More books by Blush design

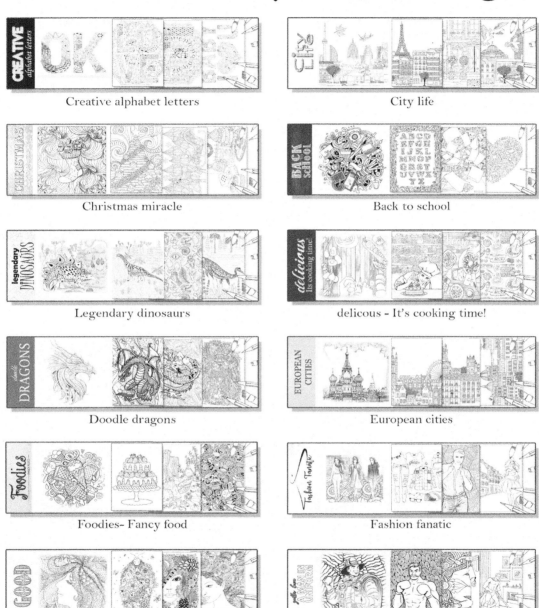

Creative alphabet letters

City life

Christmas miracle

Back to school

Legendary dinosaurs

delicous – It's cooking time!

Doodle dragons

European cities

Foodies- Fancy food

Fashion fanatic

Good hair day

Gotta love a man in uniform

www.amazon.com/blushdesign

More books by Blush design

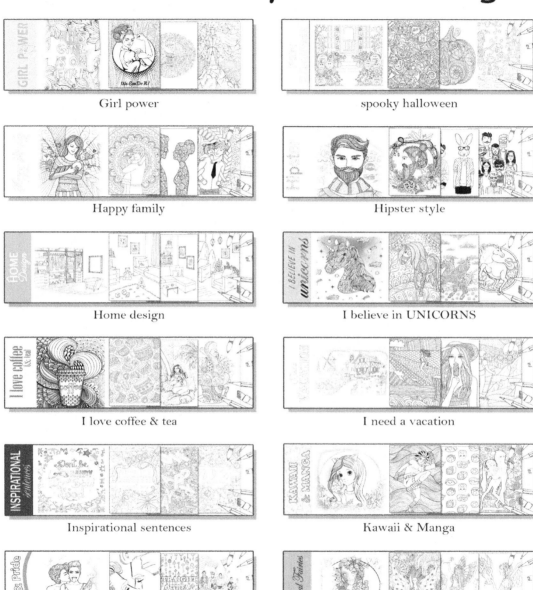

Girl power

spooky halloween

Happy family

Hipster style

Home design

I believe in UNICORNS

I love coffee & tea

I need a vacation

Inspirational sentences

Kawaii & Manga

Love & pride

Magical fairies

Find us on 📘📷 BLUSH.DESIGN.ART

More books by Blush design

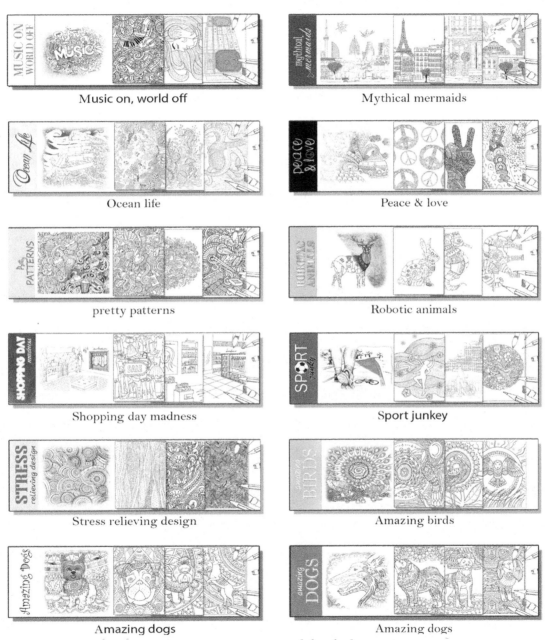

Music on, world off

Mythical mermaids

Ocean life

Peace & love

pretty patterns

Robotic animals

Shopping day madness

Sport junkey

Stress relieving design

Amazing birds

Amazing dogs

Amazing dogs

More books by Blush design

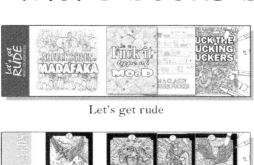

Let's get rude

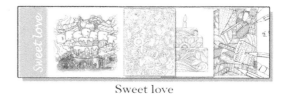

Sweet love

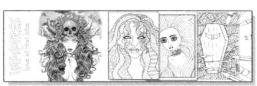

Tarot cards

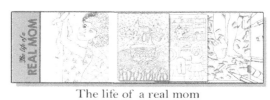

The life of a real mom

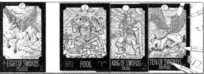

Vampires – love at first bite

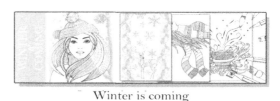

Winter is coming

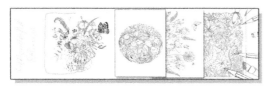

Wonderful flowers

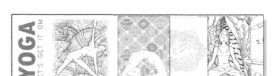

YOGA – let's get it ommm

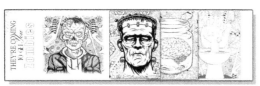

ZOMBIES– they're coming to get you

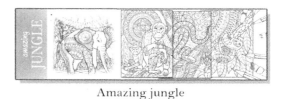

Amazing jungle

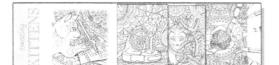

Amazing kittens

Amazing nature

Find us on 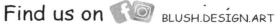 BLUSH.DESIGN.ART

More books by Blush design

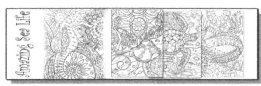

Amazing sea life

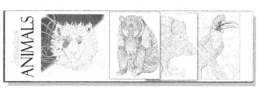

Awesome animals

Made in the USA
Middletown, DE
27 December 2022

20503204R00044